THINGS YOUR
GRANNY
SHOULD HAVE TOLD YOU

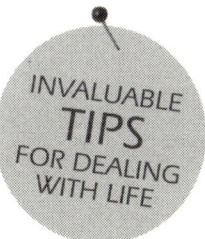

INVALUABLE
TIPS
FOR DEALING
WITH LIFE

From the popular column in the
Sunday Star-Times's Sunday magazine

HarperCollins*Publishers*

National Library of New Zealand Cataloguing-in-Publication Data

Things your Granny should have told you.
ISBN 978-1-86950-721-3
1. Home economics. 2. Life skills.
I. Sunday star times.
640.41—dc 22

First published 2008
Reprinted 2009
HarperCollins*Publishers*
(New Zealand) Limited
P.O. Box 1, Auckland

ISBN: 978 1 86950 721 3
Cover design: Natalie Winter
Cover images: Granny by Jo Tronc,
Sunday Star-Times's Sunday magazine;
floral border from Shutterstock Images
Internal text design and typesetting:
IslandBridge

Printed by Griffin Press, Australia.
70gsm Classic used by
HarperCollins*Publishers* is a natural,
recyclable product made from wood grown in
a combination of sustainable plantation and
regrowth forests. It also contains up to a
20% portion of recycled fibre. The
manufacturing processes conform to the
environmental regulations the country of
origin, Finland.

contents

Introduction   5

Etiquette
How to ...

have perfect table manners   6
be a best man   8
write a condolence letter   10
apologise   12
listen   14
be a bridesmaid   16
make an introduction   18
flirt   20
write a letter to the editor   22
host a dinner party   24
return goods to a shop   26

Self-improvement
How to ...

overcome shyness   28
speak in public   30
remember names   32
improve concentration   34
get out of debt   36
give a massage   38
become an astronaut   40
open a Swiss bank account   42
apply lipstick   44
train your dog   46

Health
How to ...

prevent motion sickness   48
have good posture   50
do the Heimlich manoeuvre   52
jog   54
make a first-aid kit   56
get a good night's sleep   58
treat a jellyfish sting   60

Clothing and jewellery
How to ...

sew on a button   62
remove pilling from clothes   64
resize a shrunken jumper   66
sew a French seam   68
iron a shirt   70
handwash clothes   72
look after pearls   74
buy a diamond   76

Gardening
How to ...

build a compost heap   78
grow tomatoes   80
care for cut flowers   82
re-pot a houseplant   84

Food and drink

How to ...

break a coconut 86
boil an egg 88
make stock 90
make a martini 92
fillet a fish 94
make tea 96
choose fruit and veg 98
taste wine 100
cook crayfish 102

Housekeeping

How to ...

clean with vinegar 104
remove stains from fabric 106
clean windows 108
fold a fitted sheet 110
deodorise your fridge 112
remove candle wax 114

DIY

How to ...

strip wallpaper 116
paint your house 118
unclog a sink drain 120
clean gutters 122
lay a brick patio 124

Car

How to ...

jump-start a car 126
buy a used car 128
change your oil 130
save petrol 132
change a car tyre 134
parallel park 136

Grammar

How to ...

use a semicolon 138
speed-read 140
use an apostrophe 142
build your vocabulary 144

Work

How to ...

handle a job interview 146
resign correctly 148

Out and about

How to ...

swing a golf club 150
light a campfire 152
bid at an auction 154
skip a stone 156
swim freestyle 158

Meet the Grannies 160

introduction

Never eat in the street, or comb your hair or apply lipstick in public. Always use a silver spoon to crack *crème brulée*, and copper-bottomed saucepans for *choux* pastry, and to be sure your crab apple jelly sets as clear as a jewel refrain from squeezing the muslin bag while it is hanging.

Part folk-lore, part home science, part etiquette, this is some of the advice I associate with my grandmothers.

In point of fact, I don't remember either of them offering direct instruction on any matter; rather we absorbed their lessons by a sensuous process of osmosis: the scent of moth balls in a warm cupboard stacked with starched bed linen and silk quilts; pantries laden with home baking; sewing rooms spilling with fabrics and button jars; gardens groaning with fruit and flowers.

They were utterly different: *Grand-mère*, elegant, refined, slightly aloof – French to the core; Grandma, small, soft and as warm as the sun porch in which she basked for many of her latter years.

Like most women of their generation they were experts in a dozen fields, raising families and running households through wars and economic slumps.

The column 'things your granny should have told you' was intended partly as a nostalgic tribute to all our grandmothers and partly as an attempt to revive some of the lost arts of home making.

It has been a favourite part of the *Sunday Star-Times*'s *Sunday Magazine* since its launch in 2003.

Cate Honoré Brett
Editor

how to

have perfect table manners

When dining at someone's home, take your cue from the host — this goes for sitting down, starting, or getting up from the table at the end.

When in a restaurant, don't start until everyone has been served, and make sure you know what's yours: your bread plate is to the left, your glassware to the right.

Some other things to think about:

● Posture
Sit up straight and don't rest your elbows on the table.

● Passing
When asked to pass something, place it on the table next to the other person rather than putting it in their hand. When asked for the salt, pass the pepper too.

● Napkins

Fold neatly in your lap and use periodically to dab your mouth, but definitely not to blow your nose. If you have to do something disgusting, excuse yourself, placing your napkin on the left side of your plate. Placing it on the right side signals you have finished.

● Utensils

Use from the outside in. If you drop one, don't crawl under the table, just ask for a replacement. When finished, place your knife and fork together diagonally on the plate with the handles facing towards you.

how to
be a best man

Being a best man is an important job. Take your cues from the groom as to what is required of you, but also check in with the bride, as she often knows more about what's going on. If you can anticipate the little things that need doing before you are asked, you'll be the best best man possible.

● **Pre-wedding**
Organise the stag do around an activity like golf, whisky tasting or big game fishing, and make sure everyone who should be is invited. Help with renting the suits or tuxes, and look after the rings prior to the service. School up on names and details of people attending and the order of service. A checklist is at www.thebestman.com.

etiquette

● **On the day**
Help the groom get dressed. Everyone should be in charge of their own suits, but bring a spare pair of socks, shoes and a belt on the day in case anyone forgets. Welcome the guests and show them where to sit (left side for groom, right for bride), and produce the rings at the appropriate time. You may also need to witness the signing of the marriage certificate.

*R*emember
Your reception speech is the most important job and is not an opportunity to get back at the groom for that wedgie or the time he stole your girlfriend.

how to
write a condolence letter

The condolence letter is a very difficult thing to write. Words are seen as an inadequate means of expression, but the formalities surrounding a death mean that silence is not an option.

The worst assumption someone can make is that such a letter will somehow compound the recipient's grief. If you feel paralysed by the fear of saying the wrong thing, try to remember that you are not trying to alleviate their pain but are offering the comfort of a connection. A simple, sincere expression of sympathy can remind the recipient that they are not alone in their grief.

Begin with a sentence that expresses sympathy for the death of their loved one. Use the word 'death' rather than a

euphemism; that way you are acknowledging the reality and not turning it into another impersonal greeting-card moment.

Include a few sentences about the deceased. Using their name, invoke a shared memory or a few words about their personality. Condolence cards are often kept as mementos of a person's life. Sign off with a sentence or two offering your continued support, particularly after the immediate formalities (such as the funeral) are over. If you offer a future phone call or visit, make sure you follow this up.

how to
apologise

Whether it's for something serious or just a minor mishap, apologising can often feel embarrassing and difficult. Fear of negative consequences such as rejection can hold us back, but having the courage to apologise always leaves both parties better off.

● The most important thing is that you must mean it. There is no point in apologising to someone if you don't care that you have hurt that person.

● Where possible, try to apologise face-to-face so you can show you are sincere. Body language is a strong indicator of how you really feel.

- The best way to show you are genuinely remorseful is to acknowledge the pain you have caused. Do more than just say 'I'm sorry'; attempt to put yourself in the other person's shoes and explain that you understand the impact your actions have had.

- If it is a situation you can remedy by doing something, offer to help.

- And remember: do not pass blame on to someone or something else — taking responsibility for your actions shows that you really do understand what you have done.

how to
listen

Larry King, the godfather of American talk-show television, once said, 'I never learned anything when I was talking.' Being a good communicator is more than just knowing what you are talking about or being a good speaker; it's learning from what other people have to say. Knowing how to listen also allows you to improve your relationships, whether at work or home, or socially.

● Pay attention to what the other person is saying. This may sound silly, but focusing on what someone is saying is often difficult, especially when your mind is running away with its own ideas. Looking them in the eye while they are talking will help you.

etiquette

- When you don't know what they are talking about, admit it. This not only keeps you focused on the conversation, but helps you to learn as well.

- If you are after certain information from a person, such as in an interview situation, help them open up by introducing topics they will be informed about and feel comfortable with.

how to
be a bridesmaid

Being a bridesmaid is often a much bigger task than it first appears. A lot of time and money can be spent helping the bride prepare for her big day, but if you bear in mind a few simple tips, stress can be kept to a minimum.

Pre-wedding

● Bridesmaids are traditionally expected to buy their own dress and shoes, but this being the case you should be able to have a say in the selection process. You at least want to be able to wear the shoes again.

● Help the maid-of-honour with the bridal-shower planning. It is often best to ask the bride what she would like and plan it around that.

etiquette

On the day

- If you are adept at public speaking and are asked to give a speech, go for it. If you feel shy, just keep it short and sincere.

- Your main job on the wedding day is to look after the bride. However, if you are unlucky enough to have a Bridezilla on your hands, just remember it's only 24 hours out of your life. Tomorrow, it's all about you again.

how to
make an introduction

Knowing how to make a proper introduction is a sign of good manners, and can also create social and business opportunities for those you are introducing. So use these suggestions and watch your popularity rise with friends and acquaintances.

● Never ignore an introduction. Whether at a party, a formal do, or just walking down the street, always introduce whomever you are with to the person or people you meet.

● If you have forgotten the name of the person you are introducing, it is far more polite to apologise and say that their name has slipped your mind than to ignore introductions altogether.

etiquette

- To aid conversation between those you are introducing, also provide some information about each person as you are giving their names, such as how you know them, or what they do for work.

- At formal functions, such as work dinner parties, introduce people using both their first and last names.

- When someone is being introduced to you, pay attention, listen to their name and focus on remembering it. This will aid in future conversations and possible introductions later.

- It is appropriate and polite in most situations to shake hands.

how to
flirt

Flirting is an often underestimated social skill that when carried out with aplomb can't help but charm others. Being a good flirt shows you have a sense of humour and are fun to be around. For some people it comes naturally, but for others it can be learned.

● First, be clear about your goal. Are you flirting to attract someone, or simply to charm them? Adjust your behaviour accordingly and make your intentions clear — don't lead them on.

● Make sure you are not hurting anyone by flirting aggressively; the person you're talking to might have a partner. Avoid corny, threatening, or overtly sexual remarks or behaviour, such as touching someone inappropriately.

etiquette

● Use engaging body language. Smile sincerely and touch the person lightly on the shoulder or arm. Stand tall and confident.

● Whatever your goal, eye contact is the key. It shows you recognise the person and are paying attention.

● Don't be afraid of starting a conversation.

● Get out of the house and visit new places to meet new people.

● Don't be put off by rejection — it happens to everyone.

how to
write a letter to the editor

Writing a letter to the editor is a great way to let people know how you feel about a topic and it adds to the crucial democratic function of free speech. Editors often receive a number of letters, so to help you get published follow these simple guidelines.

● Try to keep to the general requirements set out by the editor. These are normally written at the bottom of the letters page.

● Always stick to the word limit. If you are succinct and to the point, it is less likely that your letter will be edited in a way you don't like. It also means that readers are more likely to read it.

etiquette

● Keep vague insults to a minimum. They don't add much to the debate.

● Good grammar also helps — it means less work for the sub-editor.

● It helps if the topic is timely. Choosing something that has been mentioned in an article or is a relevant subject will help. On the other hand, if you feel very strongly about something, write a letter anyway. It is better than just complaining to your neighbour.

how to
host a dinner party

Winter is a great time to host a dinner party as most people are hibernating from the cold and will appreciate the opportunity to socialise. Follow these steps to help the evening go smoothly.

● Send out invitations with an RSVP. It's a good way to make sure of numbers and food preferences. There's no point making a roast if half the guests are vegetarian. Formal parties need a few weeks' notice, but for a casual dinner several days should be fine.

● Plan the meal well in advance. If you have questionable cooking skills, it might pay to have a more experienced friend to help you. If you want to try something new, do a test-run before the day of the party. Or else stick with a tried-and-true dish.

- Buy your fresh food as close to the day as possible — try farmers' markets for locally made produce. Find wine that is a good match for each course. Check out www.wineanswers.com for suggestions. Expect guests to bring wine — most people do nowadays. But stock up just in case.

- Leave time to prepare the meal. You don't want to be stuck in the kitchen when your friends arrive.

- Don't let your guests do the dishes, even if they offer. It's their turn to relax.

how to
return goods to a shop

Broadly speaking, you can return items only if the store is at fault or the item is faulty, not if you have changed your mind or have mistreated the item. You'll also need proof of purchase — either a receipt or a bank statement.

● If you have problems, ask to deal with the manager or owner. They are more likely to act on your concerns.

● Faulty goods (including second-hand goods and gifts) are covered by the Consumer Guarantees Act. This Act basically provides a guarantee, on behalf of the sellers and manufacturers, that goods will be of an acceptable quality.

● If it's a minor problem, the seller or maker can choose to fix the goods first. If they refuse, or the repair takes

etiquette

longer than is reasonable, you can ask for your money back or a replacement, or you can take the goods elsewhere to be fixed and be reimbursed for the repair.

● If the problem is serious, you can get your money back, get an item of similar value and type, or keep the goods and have the price reduced.

● You can expect compensation for consequential loss — say, if your faulty toaster caught fire and burned a wall.

The Ministry of Consumer Affairs (www.consumeraffairs. govt.nz) can provide more information.

how to
overcome shyness

Most people have suffered shyness at some point. The trick is to focus on feeling confident rather than trying to avoid feeling shy. Here are some tips:

● Practise being confident in private. Walk tall, with your head high, and talk firmly and with importance. You'll feel silly to begin with, but it will help.

● Imitate people who look confident and whom you respect. The new behaviours will soon feel natural.

● Think of a time or situation in which you were confident and remember how you felt then.

● Tell yourself you are confident, good-looking and interesting. Don't use negatives such as 'I'm not fat'.

self-improvement

self-improvement

● Remember other people are just as worried about what you think of them as you are of what they think of you.

● If you're meeting new people, take the focus — and pressure — off yourself by asking about them. People love it when you show an interest. The more you learn to listen, the more genuine — and less nerve-wracking — conversations will become.

● Take up an activity, such as dancing or a sport. Feeling physically good about yourself will help you project poise and confidence.

how to
speak in public

Speaking in public is a common fear. The thought of having to speak in front of a room full of people who may be bored and restless fills most of us with rising panic. Here are a few tips to ease the strain.

- It's obvious, sure, but a quick mirror-check can save the embarrassment of realising too late that your fly is unzipped or a piece of your lunch is stuck in your teeth.

- Know your material well enough to need only the main points written down.

- Begin with something to grab your audience's attention, because once you've lost it, it's difficult to wrest back.

- Don't apologise in advance for your nerves or lack of experience, as it does nothing for the audience's confidence in you. Save apologies for if something goes wrong.

- To keep your talk relevant, answer the question, 'Why should these people listen to me?' Unless you're speaking to fellow experts, they won't want to know every last detail. Keep your voice patterns and supporting materials varied, and make direct eye contact to engage as many people as possible.

- Always know the expected time frame and finish early. Keep the majority of audience questions until the end.

how to
remember names

We've all been there before — desperately trying to recall somebody's name after you've met them but coming up blank. Here are some pointers to avoid embarrassment:

● Consciously listen for the name when you're introduced and repeat it in initial conversation. For example, say the name back immediately: 'It's nice to meet you, Simon.' If that's not appropriate, repeat it a couple of times in your head.

● If a person has an unfamiliar or complicated name, make conversation about it or ask them how to spell it.

● Always use their name when saying goodbye.

● If that's not enough, create a visual reference link name. Find their most distinguishing characteristic, like blonde

hair, glasses, crooked teeth or a pointy nose.
So Simon becomes 'Simon pointy-nose' (but only
to you, of course).

- Some names are easy to remember because they mean
  something else, for example Carpenter or Fisher, and so
  can invoke a visual image on their own.

- Most other names can be broken into syllables close to
  a word — for example, Chapman could be a man with
  chapped lips, or Newton a newt that weighs a tonne.

how to
improve concentration

Improving your concentration enables you to achieve more in a shorter space of time, leaving extra hours for the things you enjoy most. Here are a few tips on boosting your concentration:

- Ascertain at what time of the day you work best and try to do the bulk of your work during this time.

- Associate one particular workspace, such as a desk, solely with working. This means you must remove anything that might distract you, such as your mobile phone or television.

- Avoid procrastination by making sure you have everything you need at your desk or workspace.

- Set a goal and a time frame for achieving it, but make sure it is realistic.

● Reward yourself with breaks when you have
  completed a certain amount, but make sure you
  take your break away from the workspace.

● Keep a notepad and pen nearby to jot down anything
  that might be distracting you — you can deal with it
  later.

● Eat well, get enough sleep and exercise regularly.

And remember, learning how to concentrate is a skill and,
as with all skills, the more you practise, the better you
become.

how to
get out of debt

We all know that getting into debt is a lot easier than getting out, but by learning how to limit what you owe you can escape the never-ending cycle.

● Meet with your bank manager and ask about consolidating your loans into one loan with a low interest rate. Consider putting all credit-card debt into this loan, then cut up your cards or cancel them. If you cannot consolidate your loans, set up a payment plan to pay off those with the highest interest rates first.

● Try to avoid new debts, such as hire-purchase agreements. If you really need an item, choose an interest-free option and make sure you pay it off before the interest-free term has expired. An automatic payment plan can help with this.

self-improvement

● Make a realistic budget and stick to it. Tell friends and family about your plan so they can support you.

● Think carefully about each item before you buy — do you need it or do you just want it?

● Write down everything you spend money on. This will make you more aware and careful of your spending habits.

how to
give a massage

Few things in life are as relaxing as a massage. It takes years to learn how to give a proper therapeutic massage, but here are some simple pointers to follow if you just want to help someone relax.

● Prepare a comfortable space. If you don't have a massage table, spread some blankets on the floor. Make sure the room is warm and the lighting is low. It's best if the person removes most of their clothes and lies face-down, under a towel. Keep their body covered except for the part you are working on.

● Warm a small amount of massage oil in your hands, then spread it over the person's back and shoulders, the area that generally retains the most tension. Begin by making broad, gentle strokes over the entire back, to

warm up the muscles. Be sure to avoid the spine
and work the muscles rather than the skin. Maintain
contact with at least one of your hands throughout the
entire massage.

- Gradually increase the pressure. The most responsive
  areas are the muscles between the neck and shoulders,
  and the lower back. Use your thumbs to apply pressure
  to precise areas. Continue over the legs, the arms
  and the feet. Avoid too much pressure on the joints,
  stomach and anywhere ticklish. Finish with a scalp
  massage.

how to
become an astronaut

- Be in top shape physically and no taller than 1.9m.

- Study something useful for an astronaut, such as aerospace engineering, maths or physics. Have a science or maths degree (a PhD would be a help).

- You can train as either a pilot or a mission specialist. Before applying as a mission pilot, you must have at least 1000 hours of being the pilot in command in a jet aircraft. A mission specialist must have at least three years' work experience.

- If accepted after a physical exam, you will train intensely for up to two years in Houston, often in low-gravity conditions, with no guarantee of ever being a rocket man or woman.

● Look at www.nasa.gov for more information, including details about how to apply.

how to
open a Swiss bank account

Should you ever want to launder money, evade the IRD or keep your assets from a greedy ex-spouse, open a Swiss bank account. The country of choice for dodgy dealings has strict secrecy laws, which means the disclosure of any account information (including whether or not it exists) is a crime. Other benefits of having your money in the world's most stable economy include the easy purchase and storage of precious metals and the ability to pay out cheques in the currency of your choice.

It's easy to open an everyday account over the internet — some banks' websites have on-line application forms. The real challenge lies in opening an infamous 'numbered account'. Originally they were intended to prevent the Gestapo from learning about illegal German foreign

deposits during the 1930s, but now they just mean no one ever need know your true identity.

But here's where it gets tricky. In order to apply for a numbered account, you must personally journey to Switzerland, armed with references and a 'legitimate reason' for the request. What constitutes a legitimate reason may vary from bank to bank, but we favour: 'I'm participating in a witness protection programme.' Even if they buy it, you'll still need a minimum deposit of NZ$38,000.

how to
apply lipstick

Applying lipstick is one of the quickest and easiest ways to feel tidy and glamorous.

- The right lipstick colour is one that suits your skin tone. If your skin has a red tinge, then go for browns and blue-based reds. If you have pale skin, opt for darker shades, and olive or dark skin will suit most colours, especially pinks and other bright shades.

- Find a lipbrush you feel comfortable using, dab it in the lipstick, then start at the top of the lip working your way to the corners. Always follow the natural shape of your lip and use short brush strokes.

self-improvement

● Lipliner can also be used for subtle definition (don't go thinking Pamela Anderson, though). Apply it around the edge of your lips before starting with the lipstick.

● A trick to ensure you don't get any lipstick outside the lipline: apply one coat, press once with a tissue, and then fill again using the original outline as a guide.

● Traditionally, lighter lipstick is worn during the day and darker shades for evening.

how to
train your dog

Getting your dog to learn a couple of basic commands will make your life easier and strengthen the bond between you. Say the commands clearly and firmly, and give praise. Also give rewards — small edible treats go down well — when they master a trick. Try to practise in a familiar environment so your dog won't be distracted. Teach one trick at a time, and expect to spend approximately 20 minutes a day on it for at least a week.

● Sit

Face your dog and point your finger at its backside, saying 'sit'. Move your dog's body into the sitting position, repeating 'sit' every few seconds. It should soon move without you touching it.

● **Stay**

Once your dog has learned 'sit', it can learn 'stay'. Tell your dog to sit, and extend your arm with your palm up like a stop signal, saying 'stay'. Repeat the word every few seconds as you slowly back away, keeping your arm up. When you are a few metres away, say 'come here' — only rewarding your dog when it stays put until you call. If it moves before then, say 'no' firmly and start again.

Note: Personal recommendations are best if you want professional help training your dog.

how to

prevent motion sickness

The green-gilled passengers who woozily disembark from the inter-island ferry are a reminder of how easily the thrill of travel can turn sour for some. Caused by sensory confusion (your mind perceives movement, but your body remains static), no one really knows why some people are more susceptible than others. But by the time symptoms like nausea or dizziness manifest, it can be too late to stop them. With motion sickness, prevention is always better than cure.

● Before you travel, take anti-nausea drugs or a herbal supplement such as ginger-root to quell nausea.

● Although it sounds flaky, gentle continuous pressure on the acupressure point on the underside of your wrist can help. There are even special wristbands you can buy at chemists which do this for you.

health

● Eat light meals and drink plenty of water before you depart. Get as much fresh air as possible when you travel. And if you're prone to travel sickness, don't travel hungover.

● Choose a seat by the window and look out at the direction you are travelling or at a fixed point on the horizon if you start feeling queasy. The most stable seats are in the middle.

● Avoid reading or knitting.

how to
have good posture

Bad posture can make you look frumpy, and can lead to headaches, back pain and fatigue. Many people have bad posture their entire lives yet don't think about the way they stand until someone calls their attention to it.

● Maintaining good posture can be challenging, but with practice it will come naturally. To practise how to stand well, do a wall test. Stand with your head, shoulders and back against a wall with your feet 12–15cm forward. Pull in your lower abdominal muscles and decrease the arch in your lower back. Push away from the wall and try to hold this position.

● Many of us spend the day at a desk, so good sitting posture is important. Ideally, buy an ergonomic chair for work. Spread your weight evenly on both hips and put

your bum against the back of the seat. Alter your chair so that your feet are flat on the floor. Try not to sit in the same position for more than 30 minutes.

- When standing, use your abdominal muscles to pull your stomach towards your back. Elongate your midsection by bringing your ribcage away from your hipbones. Pull your shoulders away from your ears, and your shoulder blades towards your spine. Relax your arms. Square your head on top of your neck and spine, and pretend there is a string attached to the top of your head pulling you upwards. If you are standing for a long period of time, shift your weight from one foot to the other.

how to
do the Heimlich manoeuvre

Since being introduced to the world in 1974 by American doctor Henry Heimlich, the Heimlich manoeuvre has been regarded as the most effective way to dislodge foreign objects from the windpipe. This basic first-aid skill is said to have saved more than 50,000 lives in the United States alone, including those of Elizabeth Taylor, Goldie Hawn, Cher and former president Ronald Reagan.

● From behind, wrap your arms around the waist of the person choking. Make a fist and place the thumb side against the upper abdomen, below the ribcage and above the navel.

● Press your fist into the upper abdomen with your other hand, with a quick upward thrust. Repeat until the object is expelled.

health

● If your victim is unconscious or you can't reach your arms around them, lay them on their back and straddle their hips to perform the manoeuvre.

● Do not pound a choking person on the back, as this may cause the object to lodge further.

Source: The Heimlich Institute, www.heimlichinstitute.org

how to
jog

The right shoes will be your most important item. Buy them from a specialist sports-shoe store, where the staff can recommend the best pair for your running style. They should ask to see an old pair of your shoes, or at least see you run a small distance. Shop around — the best shoes for you might not be the most expensive.

● Warm up by walking for a few minutes and then stretching. Do the same to cool down. Wear a short-sleeved top and shorts. If it's cold, cover your limbs and wear a hat and gloves. Jog at a comfortable pace; you should be warm and breathing quickly, but still able to talk. Have your arms bent by your side and hands gently curled, letting them swing naturally with your body. Make sure your heel lands on the ground first,

then roll your foot forward and push off from the toe. Be guided by your natural stride.

● Breathe naturally through your nose and mouth. Some people like to breathe in through the nose and out through the mouth, but don't force yourself to breathe in any particular way as it can quickly tire you out.

● Vary the terrain you run through to increase fitness, which will decrease your risk of injury. It's better to run on softer surfaces, such as dirt or grass, to minimise jarring of your joints. Don't lean back when jogging down hills, and use your arms to power yourself up hills.

how to
make a first-aid kit

Having a first-aid kit is one of the most basic steps you can take to care for yourself and those around you. You can buy ready-made kits from organisations such as St Johns and the Red Cross, but if you have most of the items already, you can put together your own. Make two — one for the home and one for the car. Include:

● tissues for general cleaning, and sterilised gauze swabs for cleaning wounds

● different-shaped sticking plasters for shallow cuts or grazes, and larger non-sticky dressings for bigger wounds

● a roll of adhesive strapping to hold dressings in place

● stretch bandages to strap limbs

● a triangular bandage to make into a shoulder sling

health

- scissors, tweezers and safety pins

- plastic bags to use as an ice-pack covering or for dirty bandages

- latex gloves to prevent cross-infection

- a first-aid information sheet — including instructions for CPR

- painkillers for aches and pains

- antiseptic cream or wipes

- burn cream or gel

- for the car: a notebook and pen to record information at the scene of an accident.

how to
get a good night's sleep

Insomnia can be very frustrating. The following suggestions may help you get a good night's sleep:

● Sleep in a dark, quiet room that is reasonably cool, using extra blankets instead of heating to stay warm. If absolute quiet doesn't suit you, soft background noise can help — try music with no discernible melody, such as a baroque classical piece.

● Worrying is the most common barrier to falling asleep. Keep a pen and paper by your bed and jot down any thoughts or concerns you might have before you go to bed. This can help slow your mind down.

● Get into a regular sleep pattern. Get up at the same time each day, even if you have had a late night. Avoid

napping during the day, and don't take sleeping pills as they can disrupt normal habits.

● Having a glass of warm milk before bed is sound grandmotherly advice — dairy products contain tryptophan, which is thought to induce serotonin and, in turn, sleep. Avoid eating, exercise and stimulants (alcohol, caffeine and nicotine) for at least four hours before bedtime.

● If you can't sleep after 30 minutes, get out of bed and do something like read, watch television or take a bath. Don't expose yourself to bright light. If you're still awake at 5 a.m., simply get up and get on with your day. If your insomnia persists, try a stress-management programme or meditation.

how to
treat a jellyfish sting

Oh, it's nice to be beside the seaside, but beware the traps within. Venomous marine animals can cause everything from mild pain to serious illness. If you get bitten or stung by a jellyfish at the beach:

● Wash the area with soap, or disinfectant and water.

● Remove any stings or tentacles attached to the skin.

● If swelling starts, apply ice and cover with a sticking plaster (don't apply ice to fingers or toes).

● If there is pain or tenderness, soak the area in hot (not burning) water for 15–20 minutes and take pain relief.

health

● See a doctor immediately if an allergic reaction (rash, temperature, swelling of the face or neck, difficulty breathing) develops.

● DON'T apply methylated spirits or vinegar. Vinegar is only effective for Australian Box Jellyfish stings; it can make other bites and stings more painful.

how to

sew on a button

When replacing a lost button, make sure the new one fits through the buttonhole before you start.

● Take a needle and doubled-up thread about 40cm long. Attach the thread to the fabric by making a series of small stitches over the top of one another on the underside of the fabric while holding the loose end. You can use a knot instead but it is not as tidy.

● Put the button where you want it and place a matchstick or toothpick on top of the button.

● Sew the button on by going in and out through each hole six to eight times with the needle and thread, making sure the matchstick or toothpick sits under the loops.

clothing and jewellery

- Remove the matchstick or toothpick. Pull the button up to expose the space between the button and fabric (called the shank) and wind the thread around the shank a few times for extra strength.

- Pull the needle back through to the underside of the fabric and make another series of small stitches to secure the thread. Use scissors to cut off any loose ends.

how to
remove pilling from clothes

How annoying it can be to buy a gorgeous new top only to have it grow a crop of little fuzzies after only a few wears. Woven or knitted fabrics are the most likely culprits, but short of never buying another angora sweater, here are some tips for keeping your garment looking new.

● Pilling can't be completely avoided, but you can minimise the nobbly effect by turning your pill-prone clothes inside out before washing. Do a gentle handwash and hang them to dry.

● Pilling is caused by rubbing, so the less abrasion the garment goes through, the better.

clothing and *jewellery*

● Skimming a safety razor over the fabric can remove pills. However, it's not ideal because you risk cutting the fabric.

● The other options are to buy either a special de-pilling comb, or an electric pill remover which works much like a razor.

● Some people swear by the Sweater Stone, made of pumice, for removing pills. Go to www.sweaterstone. com.

how to
resize a shrunken jumper

First of all, don't despair. You may yet be able to breathe new life into that favourite woolly knit.

- Fill a basin with warm water, squirt in some baby shampoo (Mustela is very good) and give the water a good swish.

- Put jumper on top of the water. Let it sink by itself, and then leave for about 15 minutes.

- Remove the jumper — but do not wring — and put it in a spare container while you re-fill basin with clear water.

- Again, lay the jumper on top and let it sink to rinse.

- Remove jumper, place on a dry towel and roll up to soak up most of the moisture.

clothing and *jewellery*

● Lay jumper on a dry towel on a flat surface and gently start to pull it back into shape.

● Continue to reshape it as it dries. Have patience.

● If all else fails, ask the skilled knitter in your family or circle of friends to forgive you and knit something new.

how to
sew a French seam

A French seam is particularly suitable for delicate fabrics and for people with delicate skins because the seam encloses the raw edges into itself. This makes it ideal for sheer fabrics that might not handle zigzagging or overlocking well, as well as baby wear.

- Start with the wrong sides of the fabric together. Sew a fine seam. Trim edges if you feel so inclined.

- Unfold with right sides up. Press the seam open.

- With the right sides together, fold the fabric along the seam line. Press again, so you have a sharp crease and no buckling.

clothing *and* *jewellery*

- Sew a new seam that completely encases the original seam. Make sure you don't have any frayed edges exposed.

- Unfold with wrong sides up. Press entire length of seam flat to one side.

- This is not an exercise that you should hurry. Patience, precision, a sharp eye — and sharp scissors — help.

how to
iron a shirt

If there's one thing that can be guaranteed in the minefield that is office politics, it is this: no one will ever be impressed by a wrinkled shirt. As the adorable Carson from TV's *Queer Eye for the Straight Guy* has aptly demonstrated, good ironing technique is like prayer — it can change your life.

Regardless of the fabric, you'll get the best result by ironing shirts while they're damp, before the wrinkles set in. Before you start, test the fabric to make sure it won't melt or scorch by ironing a small patch on an inside shirt-tail.

● Place the collar flat on the board, wrong side up, and press from the outer points toward the centre. Turn over and repeat.

clothing and _jewellery_

● Press the inside of the cuff, and then the outside. Iron the sleeves, making sure the crease is aligned and any gathers are flattened with the tip of the iron. Press the yoke (shoulder panel) on the wide end of the board.

● Lay the back of the shirt flat and press. Do the side seams from the inside of the shirt and then the outside.

● Iron the front pocket and then the front panels, applying extra pressure between the buttons and buttonholes. Hang shirt to dry if it's still slightly damp.

how to
handwash clothes

Aside from 'iron with a press cloth', 'hand wash' is the most pesky instruction you can find on a clothing label. It's tempting to pretend you never saw it and bang the delicate darling in the washing machine. Don't do it. It doesn't matter how gentle your Gentle Annie is, it ain't worth taking the risk. Grab a bucket and accept your fate.

- Place a bucket in the tub and fill it with cold water. Add a gentle clothes detergent.

- Put the pesky item of clothing into the bucket, plunge your hands in and imagine you are a washing machine. Really get into character. Agitate the garment by swooshing it round and round. Go to town on any especially stinky or stained spots by rubbing other parts of the material against it.

clothing *and* *jewellery*

● Let the clothing sit in the soapy water for 10 minutes.

● Remove the clothing from the water and pour the contents down the drain. Re-fill the bucket with cold water, running each part of the fabric under the tap as you do it. When the bucket is full, whack the garment back underwater and start your agitating motion again.

● Empty the bucket and repeat until there are no suds on the clothes or in the water.

how to
look after pearls

Most pearls these days are cultured, which means they have a thicker coating of the shiny, iridescent nacre than wild pearls. But pearls are still more fragile than other gemstones, and need special attention.

● To minimise contact with harmful things like perfume, make-up, perspiration and hairspray, make sure your pearls are the last thing you put on and the first thing you take off. Take off pearl rings when you wash your hands or put hand cream on.

● Wipe with a damp cloth to remove body oils, and store in a soft pouch or wrap away from harder jewellery that might scratch or dent them.

● Pearls need restringing often because the thread collects dirt and discolours. If you wear them more than

once a week, restring them every one to two years; if less, every three to four years. String them with knots in between, so that they don't touch at the drill hole, which is the weakest point. Most jewellers give a free appraisal as to whether your pearls need restringing.

● Pearls are organic substances containing about two percent water. Extreme heat or dry conditions can cause them to crack or lose lustre.

● Only use jewellery cleaner that is labelled 'safe for pearls'. Don't clean them with abrasive brushes or cloths. Lay them flat to dry.

how to
buy a diamond

If diamonds are a girl's best friend, then the purchase of one should be done with care. Before heading to the jeweller, familiarise yourself with the four Cs: cut, colour, clarity, carat.

● **Cut**

When a diamond is cut correctly, light is refracted well and the diamond will dazzle.

● **Colour**

Diamonds are almost entirely composed of carbon, but do contain traces of other elements, which can add colour. A totally colourless diamond is best because light can pass through it easily.

clothing and *jewellery*

● **Clarity**

Most diamonds contain small impurities known as 'inclusions'. As inclusions can interfere with the light passing through a diamond, the fewer inclusions the more beautiful the diamond. Major ones will appear as cloudiness to the naked eye.

● **Carat**

The diamond's weight is measured in carats.

The very lucky can afford a large, perfectly cut, colourless, flawless diamond. The rest of us need to decide how we want to spend our money — on a bigger diamond with more impurities or a smaller, more perfect stone? Take your time deciding: diamonds hang around for a long time.

how to
build a compost heap

- First make, or get, a bin. Simple suggestions include netting wound around four corner posts, or a rigid plastic bin with a well-fitting lid.

- Start your heap with a base of mixed, finely chopped organic material (such as leaves and twigs), which provides adequate aeration for the heat. Follow with a thin layer of soil.

- Add any healthy organic material that comes to hand, such as: vegetable peelings, egg shells, tea (leaves and bags), coffee grindings, shredded paper, grass and garden clippings.

- Do not add any diseased or invasive plants.

gardening

- Build your heap up as you go, but remember to turn it. This stops it going sour and keeps it aerated.

- When the heap is at optimum height, cover with a thin layer of soil and black polythene sheeting to retain the heat.

- Keep moist, but not wet, at all stages.

- Compost should be ready to use in six to eight weeks in summer and three to four months in winter.

how to
grow tomatoes

There's nothing quite like the taste of home-grown tomatoes — vine-ripened and pungent, they are an essential part of summer salads. Spring is the ideal season to plant them, as tomato plants need at least three months of warm, frost-free weather.

- Tomatoes should thrive in any rich, well-drained soil as long as they are getting plenty of sunshine and are sheltered from the wind. They can also be grown in pots or planters (especially the smaller varieties) using potting mix.

- Plant seedlings about 30 to 40cm apart, in well-fertilised soil up to about 2cm up the stem.

gardening

- Tall varieties will need stakes for support. Plants also need to be pruned regularly to encourage more energy into the fruit and stem. Do this by removing lateral stems when they appear.

- When the plant has six or seven good tomatoes, pinch off the growing tip.

- Regular watering and fertilising is essential with a fast-growing plant like this.

- Pick your tomatoes when they are ripe but still firm, to encourage the plant to produce more fruit.

how to
care for cut flowers

Flowers continue to live after they are cut from the plant. With a little attention they can last a long time.

- It's best to harvest flowers in the morning when it is cool and they are full of moisture and nutrients. Stems with multiple blooms should have about half the buds open, whereas flowers with one per stem should be fully open. Cut the stem with a sharp, clean pair of clippers on the diagonal — this helps the flower get more water. Take care not to crush the stem. Put the flowers in water immediately.

- When it is time to put your flowers into a vase, re-cut the stem diagonally under water. Varieties with hard stems benefit from having their cut ends plunged into hot water first. Remove any foliage that will be under water in the vase and add a flower preservative to the water — this helps to make hard, or alkaline, water more acidic. You can make your own preservative by mixing 1 tsp sugar, 1 tsp household bleach and 2 tsp lemon or lime juice into 1 litre of water.

- Don't overcrowd the vase and keep the water replenished. Place the arrangement in a cool place, out of draughts and direct sunlight, and away from ripening fruit and vegetables, as they produce ethylene, which shortens the life of flowers. At the first sign of wilting, re-cut the stems under running water.

how to
re-pot a houseplant

If your plants are beginning to look a little sad, they may need to be moved to larger premises. Although certain species will bloom only if root-bound, most need to be re-potted every two or three years.

- Choose a slightly larger container than the current pot, and cover the drainage hole with gauze or a piece of ceramic to stop the soil falling out. Use a potting mix that is not too light to hold water, nor so rich that it will encourage fungus. Put an inch or two of mix in the bottom.

- Water the plant in its original pot one hour before you take it out. Turn the pot over and tap it so the plant slides out, and gently tease out the outer roots.

gardening

● Put the plant in the new pot, adding soil around it until the soil is level with the base of the stem. Water sparingly and keep the plant in a shadier location than usual for about a week, giving it time to adjust.

*R*emember

Only re-pot during spring or summer while the plant is actively growing. Do not re-pot ailing or dormant plants, or those starting to flower. For plants in large containers, remove the top four or five centimetres of soil and replace this with fresh mix every other year.

how to
break a coconut

You don't need me to tell you that fresh is best. Coconut — the milk and "meat" — is no exception. Here, then, is how to crack open a coconut and enjoy the fruits of your labour.

- You'll need a nail (or screwdriver), a hammer, a towel and a bowl.

- Lay the towel on a flat, hard surface and place a coconut on top. Pierce one or two of the small, dark spots on the coconut (there are usually three, about the size of a 10 cent piece) using the hammer, or screwdriver, and nail. Pierce the shell through the meat and no more.

- Remove the nail and drain the coconut over the bowl. Chill the milk and enjoy mixed with rum later.

- Put the coconut back on the towel. Then strike forcefully with the hammer.

- The smaller the shards, the easier to remove the meat from the husk (with a sharp, wide-bladed knife, or by grating).

- This is work for the outdoors: physical but worth it.

how to
boil an egg

Many New Zealanders have childhood memories of dunking toast soldiers into gooey soft-boiled eggs. For other hard-boiled types, this simple meal was spread on buttered toast or simply peeled and eaten on its own. But make no mistake: these are not dishes for children alone.

To boil an egg, place eggs in a small saucepan, so they don't bounce around too much, and just cover with cold water. Use a high heat until boiling, and then reduce to a gentle simmer for:

- **3 minutes**   to get a really soft-boiled egg
- **4 minutes**   the white is just set and yolk is gooey
- **5 minutes**   the white and yolk are perfectly set, with a slightly squidgy centre
- **6 minutes**   hard-boiled.

Run immediately under cold water to ensure they don't overcook and develop a black ring.

If the eggs are less than four days old, allow an extra 30 seconds — the older the egg, the larger the air pocket in the wide end of the egg will be. To test, put the egg in a glass of water. If it is very fresh it will rest horizontally, if it is around a week old it will tilt up slightly, and if it is stale it will float vertically.

how to
make stock

For a tasty, fragrant stock that makes a great base for soups, stews or risottos, make it yourself from scratch. The world's best chefs have been doing it for centuries.

The procedure is basically the same for all stocks: bring the ingredients to the boil, skim any foamy scum off the top, simmer, then strain.

Stock can be frozen in plastic containers or ice trays, or stored in the fridge for a couple of days.

● Chicken
500g of chicken parts (back, neck, wings and bones), 1 litre of water, a carrot, an onion, a celery stalk and a handful of peppercorns, 2 whole cloves, parsley sprigs and a large bay leaf. Simmer 1 hour.

food and *drink*

Vegetable
A couple each of onions, carrots, celery stalks, parsnips
and unpeeled garlic cloves, plus 8 white mushrooms,
2 litres of water, bay leaves and thyme. Simmer 1 hour.

Beef
2kg roasted beef bones, 3 litres water, an onion,
3 carrots, parsley sprigs, a few peppercorns, 4 garlic
cloves, a bay leaf, thyme and 2 cloves. Simmer 4 hours.

Fish
2kg of fish skeletons, including well-scaled heads,
4 litres of water, 1 cup white wine, a squeeze of
lemon, an onion, celery, parsley sprigs, thyme and
peppercorns. Simmer 2 hours.

how to
make a martini

The martini is a truly iconic drink, representative of all things suave and cool. And all grown-ups should know how to mix a good one — what if James Bond drops by? Of course, there are many variations on the classic gin and vermouth combo — and do you shake or do you stir? Do you throw in an olive or go with a twist? As with most beverages, personal preference should dictate.

- Shake 50ml gin and 15ml dry vermouth in a cocktail shaker full of ice. Strain into a chilled martini glass and garnish with an olive (or three), a twist of lemon rind or a cocktail onion for a 'Gibson'. For a sweet martini, replace the dry vermouth with a sweeter Italian version.

- Unlike Bond, purists may want their martini stirred. If this is this case, use a long metal cocktail spoon to gently

stir the gin, vermouth and ice, and then strain.
Stirring prevents the gin 'bruising' or becoming aerated,
and the resulting drink is not as cold.

● A vodka martini simply sees the gin replaced by good
quality vodka. For fruit variations, a vodka base is
usually best — just add your favourite fruity spirit
instead of the vermouth.

how to
fillet a fish

After gutting, cleaning and scaling your fish, it's time to fillet it. You'll need a cutting board or flat surface to work on and a sharp, narrow boning knife (never a serrated or electric knife).

● Hold the fish by the head (if it's still got one!) and slice into it behind the gill. Stop when you reach the backbone and turn the knife until it's flat against it, with the sharp edge facing the tail. Carefully cut along the fish, using the spine as a guide until the knife slides out at the tail-end.

● Peel the fillet back with one hand while cutting the flesh away from the backbone using small slicing motions. Don't try to cut too much away in one stroke; instead, use many small cuts, guiding the knife along any bony structures and removing the flesh.

food and *drink*

● Turn the fish over and repeat on the other side.

● At this stage, two sets of bones will remain in the fillet. You should be able to see the ribcage: cut this away by sliding the knife in between it and the meat. Using your fingers, find the pin bones that run through the centre of the fillet and pull them out with tweezers or pliers.

● Remove the skin from the fillet by turning it skin-side down and wiggling the knife along between the skin and the meat, leaving as little flesh as possible attached. If the skin is difficult to grasp, try making a small hole in one end of it to hook your finger into. If you are filleting flatfish remember that the bones are aligned a little differently and you will need to remove two fillets on each side.

how to
make tea

For most, it's as natural as blinking — throw a bag in a cup, pour in water, add milk. But the experts insist that making a cup of tea properly is worth the effort.

- Start with fresh cold water. Pre-boiled water loses its oxygen and can give tea a flat taste. If water from the tap doesn't taste good on its own, it won't make a good cup of tea.

- Warm a clean teapot by swirling some boiling water around it and then tipping it out. Add one teaspoon of loose-leaf tea for each person and an extra one 'for the pot'. For black and herb teas, use water that has been boiling well for a few seconds. For green tea, some experts recommend using water just off boiling so that it doesn't taste bitter.

food and *drink*

● Cover the teapot with a cosy and let it draw for 3–5 minutes for green or black tea, and up to 6 for herbal. Go by the clock and not the colour, as colour is not always a reliable measure of strength.

● Connoisseurs advocate adding milk before pouring the tea so that the milk isn't scalded. Start with less milk in the cup so that you can add more if the tea is too strong.

● If you must use a tea bag, look for the bigger-leafed brands that don't just use the dusty leftovers. Squeeze the bag to get out the most flavoursome droplets.

how to
choose fruit and veg

Any food lover will tell you that the way to a person's heart is through delicious food. Knowing how to spot fresh, ripe fruit and vegetables will mean you get the best flavour and nutrition for your money — and your friends and family will love you for it.

- Try to buy in-season, locally grown produce, as it will be fresher.

- Avoid supermarket fruit and veg, which are often sprayed with water to give the appearance of freshness. Chemicals may also be used to prolong shelf life.

- A better bet are farmers' markets and local greengrocers, particularly if they have a high product turnover. Make

friends with your local greengrocer, so he/she can help you pick the best produce. Fresh produce should look pristine and tight-skinned. Avoid anything that is limp and tired-looking or has brown spots and mould.

- If you are wondering whether to buy organic or not (and can afford to), use raw carrots as a taste test — they really show up the difference.

- If you're not sure at first, shop with a friend who knows what to look for so you can pick up some tips.

how to
taste wine

Pick a medium-sized wine glass with a rim that is
narrower than its base — this is the best shape to hold
the wine's aroma. Fill it to just below the widest part of the
glass and tilt it slightly against a white background to look
at the true colour of the wine. The wine should be clear and
bright and never cloudy.

● Sniff the wine and note your first impressions. Swirl
the wine gently in the glass, maximising the interaction
between the air and the wine's surface, and take
a couple more long, controlled sniffs of the wine.
Think about the difference (if any) before and after
swirling. Ask yourself: What is my first impression? Is it
dominated by fruit smells or something else? Is it easy
to identify or is it a mixture of things ('complexity')? Wine

should never smell vinegary or mouldy, although 'earthy' can be OK.

● Next, taste the wine by taking a small mouthful and moving it around your mouth. Breathe a little air across the wine to intensify the flavours. Try to describe what you taste and listen to what others are saying. Pay attention to not just the initial taste, but the flavours that linger after you have swallowed — this is called the 'finish'.

● Every person has a different palate. In order to familiarise yourself with your own palate and get better at describing what you taste, you need to practise. Which with wine is never a difficult thing.

how to
cook a crayfish

It's a regular fixture in all the top restaurants, but one of the best ways to enjoy crayfish or rock lobster is *al fresco* at home in the summertime.

To ensure your cray is the freshest possible, it must be caught or bought live and killed just before cooking, preferably on the same day.

For many home cooks this conjures up gruesome images of desperate crustaceans clambering out of boiling pots on the stovetop. But by freezing a cray for a couple of hours in a freezer or iced salt water, you can send them into a blissful slumber, putting a knife through their head with a clear conscience.

food *and* *drink*

● **To boil**

Keep the cray in salted boiling water for about
10–12 minutes or until their shells turn a bright orange
colour. Put in cold water immediately afterwards to
arrest the cooking process.

● **To grill**

Cut the cray in half length-wise, baste with a delicate
marinade, and grill flesh-side up until the flesh turns
opaque.

● **To roast or barbecue**

Cut in half length-wise, brush flesh with butter and roast
flesh-side down at 200°C in the oven or on the barbie for
eight to 10 minutes or until just cooked through.

how to
clean with vinegar

Before antiseptic spray, antibacterial wipes, pine-scented, lemon-fortified and forest-fragranced disinfectants, there was vinegar. Not that bourgeois balsamic muck, with its grandiose ambitions of accompanying breads, but good, honest white vinegar.

The sagacious liquid is a true friend to domesticity: cheap, versatile and environmentally friendly, it's vivacious with germs as well as stains.

● Dilute with water (½ cup of vinegar to 4 litres of water) and it's a window and floor cleaner.

● Remove watermarks in the toilet by pouring in 2 cups of vinegar. Leave to soak overnight, then flush.

● Some fabric softeners can stain 100 percent polyester garments. Instead, add half a cup of vinegar to the final rinse.

● For a great little furniture polish, add ½ teaspoon of light olive oil and ¼ cup of white vinegar to a litre of water.

● Freshen the air by mixing 1 teaspoon of baking soda, 1 tablespoon of vinegar and 2 cups of water. When the mixture stops foaming, mix well, pour into an atomizer bottle and spray away.

how to
remove *stains* from fabric

The average household cupboard has an arsenal of solutions for all types of fabric stains. Although it's a drag, always test the cleaner on a patch of hidden fabric before you start. Blot or dab the stain on the wrong side of the fabric to make sure it doesn't get worked further in. And, of course, catching the stain while it is fresh will make it much easier to remove. Here are a few tricks to try:

● **Alcohol (or meths)**   For grass stains, adhesive tape on non-synthetic fabric, candle-wax residue, ballpoint pen or correction fluid.

● **Ammonia**   Diluted in water, it can be used on perspiration stains, pre-soaked blood stains, lipstick, makeup and deodorant.

housekeeping

- **Baking soda**   Removes odours, so dissolve ¼ cup in a bucket of water to soak smelly socks or gym gear before washing.

- **Lemon juice**   Squeeze on spots on white clothes and leave in the sun before washing.

- **Shampoo**   Good for makeup and the grubby ring around shirt collars.

- **Soda water**   A great all-rounder for fresh stains. Blot and wash as normal.

- **Turps**   Sponged gently onto fabric, it dissolves oils and fats. Use on motor oil and oil-based paints, or fat residues from milk or ice cream.

how to
clean windows

Many people have their own secret tips and tricks for cleaning mirrors and windows, but the following is the cheapest, most reliable chemical-free method, and it has been used forever.

- Mix 1 cup of white vinegar in a bucket of hot water. (Alternatively, you can use a capful of ammonia or a store-bought treatment. But be careful, these can be corrosive, so wear gloves and old clothes.) Use a clean sponge dipped into the water to clean the windows, making sure to rub the dirtier bits in the corners.

- Scrunch up newspaper and use this to dry the window; a bit of elbow grease and circular motions often do the trick. Wear gloves, otherwise the newsprint will leave your hands black.

housekeeping

- For hard-to-reach windows, use a squeegee with an extension handle.

- Put vinegar in a spray bottle to clean mirrors. Just spray and wipe with newspaper or paper towels.

- To keep your bathroom mirrors from steaming up, rub with a dry bar of soap then scrub clean with a cloth.

how to
fold a fitted sheet

Wrinkly rolls of fitted sheets take up so much room in your linen cupboard that it pays to learn how to fold them flat. There is a trick to it.

● Take your fitted sheet and place your hand in the top right corner. Slip the left top corner over this hand, too, like a glove.

● Arrange the sheet full length on a flat surface and then tackle the bottom two corners, placing them like a glove over your hand in the same way as the top two.

● Now tackle the mid-section by folding the sheet lengthwise into a long rectangle.

● Finish by folding from bottom to top into a neat square or two and stack it away.

how to
deodorise your fridge

You should clean your fridge regularly, switching off the power first (transfer food to chilly bins while your fridge is out of action). Remove contents, shelves and baskets. Wash the latter in warm (not hot) water with detergent. If an odour remains, try the following:

● Leave a saucer of vanilla extract in the empty fridge for a few days.

● Sprinkle baking soda onto plates, and place on each shelf in the empty, unplugged fridge for a few days. Leave the door open.

housekeeping

- Spread kitty litter or freshly ground coffee onto shallow dishes and leave on the fridge shelves, with the fridge running and the door closed, for several days.

- If all else fails, it could be the fridge drains or pan, or the insulation. You might need a service call.

how to
remove candle wax

● **From your deck**

First scrape away solid wax, then place brown paper over the stain and iron with a hot iron (you may need to use an extension cord) until the paper absorbs the melted wax. This may take a couple of attempts.

● **From a tablecloth**

Scrape off with a fingernail or plastic knife, then sandwich the cloth between layers of brown or kitchen paper and iron until all the wax has been absorbed. If it's all over the sofa, try the iron and brown paper method, but only on fabric, not leather or vinyl.

● **From a concrete bench or floor**
Rent a commercial steamer from a DIY shop and
steam until wax evaporates.

● **To remove candle-holder build-up**
Put holder in the freezer for an hour or two and you'll be
able to remove the wax in a lump. Or put it in the oven
on low until the wax melts. Handle with gloves; it will be
very hot.

how to
strip wallpaper

When it's time to get rid of the worn-out old wallpaper that's been lurking in your laundry since the 'seventies, don't be put off by thoughts of drop cloths and dungarees. With the right tools and planning, mess can be minimised, and the resulting bare surface can be immensely satisfying.

Before you begin, you'll need cloths, chemical stripper (Resene's Metylan wallpaper remover works well), a scoring tool, a scraper with spare blades, and some household detergent.

● Clear away any furniture from the area and put down a drop cloth.

● Score (make small rips) along the surface using the scoring tool.

diy

- Apply the stripper according to the packet directions and allow it to soften the paper.

- Scrape off the paper. It's easier if you hold your scraper at a 45° angle to the wall, but take care not to gouge into the surface. Have extra stripper handy to attack stubborn bits.

- When the last scrap of paper is gone, clean away any residue with a diluted household cleaner.

- To prepare the surface for re-decorating, fill any holes with putty and sand smooth.

how to
paint your house

It's the bane of every homeowner — the 10-yearly house paint. For some, the thought of donning splattered overalls and sanding till their eyes itch perched atop a flimsy ladder makes them hire a professional. For the stalwart DIYers, here are some tips to get started:

● Trim shrubs and trees away from the house. Remove any fixtures that might get in the way of the painting.

● Give the exterior a good clean, especially in those hard-to-reach places. Attack mildew with diluted bleach and a scrubbing brush.

● Scrape and sand any areas which are peeling or cracking, and wipe with a damp rag.

diy

- Set nails below wood surface with a nail punch, fill hole with masonry filler and sand smooth.

- Prime all bare wood and leave to dry overnight.

- Paint the house exterior from the top down. Then paint the woodwork from the top down. Always paint the windows from the inside out — first the sash, then the sides, top and bottom, and then the outer moulding.

- Paint west-facing walls in the morning and east-facing walls in the afternoon, as wet paint will blister if left to dry in the full sun.

how to
unclog a sink drain

      Before you call a plumber to come and unblock your sink, there are a couple of things any self-respecting DIYer should have a go at first:

● If you're lucky, pouring a kettle of boiling water down the drain will dissolve any greasy bits and send your blockage on its way.

● Alternatively, place a plunger over the plug-hole and partially fill the sink with water to cover. If you have a double sink or an overflow opening, plug with a wet rag. Plunge vigorously up and down, keeping the seal.

● If that doesn't work, remove and clean the U-shaped pipe under the sink (the 'trap'). Wearing rubber gloves and eye protection, place a bucket under the trap to

catch whatever falls out. Using a wrench or slip-joint pliers, unscrew the metal slip-nuts a half-turn or so, and loosen them by hand. Scrape out any blockage and replace the trap, being careful not to over-tighten the nuts.

- If the clog still won't budge, try an auger or 'snake'. This tool is like a narrow, coiled spiral snake, with a handle and crank on one end. Push the snake into the drain and crank it into the clog. Parts of the blockage should break up and flush through the drain, or else it should come out attached to the snake when you remove it.

how to
clean gutters

Gutters are a necessity you never really consider until they're blocked, overflowing and causing a major flood around your house.

However, if you climb up to clean them out regularly, this will never be a problem.

● Aim to give your gutters some attention twice a year. If you have lots of deciduous trees around your house, make sure you clean them at the end of autumn or when the trees have lost almost all their leaves.

● Use a ladder, making sure you don't damage your guttering when you lean it against it. Wearing rubber gloves, scoop out as much of the debris as you can into

a bucket, and fix any cracks or loose nails along the way that need attention. Hose out the smaller bits of dirt and grit.

● If the water doesn't flow out freely, take the downspout joint apart from the gutter. Spray water through it. Stubborn clogs may have to be removed with an auger or a 'snake' by cranking the coil into the clog and pulling it out. To reattach the joint, scrape the old adhesive off and apply some new silicone sealant to keep it watertight.

how to
lay a brick patio

A simple, bricked patio is a great place to while away summer days — think small and it'll be quick to do.

- Lay out the shape of your patio using a garden hose, and hammer stakes into the ground around the perimeter every half-metre or so. (Rectangular shapes are easiest as they don't require brick-cutting.) Dig out about 20cm of grass and topsoil, making the edges completely vertical.

- Make the surface slightly higher in the middle to prevent water pooling. Half-fill the bed with gravel or concrete sand, tamping it down firmly.

- Run wooden or plastic strapping around the border to give the bricks support. Screw the strapping securely to

the stakes. If you need it to go around curves, saw partway through the wood every couple of centimetres and it should bend like a big comb.

- If you want a border, stand bricks facing inwards, so their narrow edge shows at the surface.

- Cover the gravel with stone dust and lay the rest of the bricks in the pattern you want, tamping each level with a rubber mallet. Spread stone dust over the bricks and sweep it into the cracks. Spray water over it and the dust should harden.

- Pull the stakes and strapping out a week later to ensure the bricks have settled.

how to
jump-start a car

Having your own jumper leads can save you the hassle of being stranded with a flat battery. But they must be used properly – if there's any doubt about using your equipment, it's best to call in the experts.

● Check that the batteries in both cars are the same (6 volt or 12 volt). Park the cars close together, but not touching, in neutral or park. Make sure both car ignitions and all electrical equipment are switched off.

● Connect the red jumper lead to the positive terminal (marked '+' or 'pos') of the flat battery, and then the other end to the positive terminal of the live battery.

● Connect the black lead to the negative terminal of the live battery, and then the other end to the negative terminal of the dead battery.

car

● Ensuring the leads are away from any moving parts of either vehicle, start the car with the live battery and then after a few minutes start the vehicle with the flat battery (if it doesn't start, consult a mechanic).

● Allow both engines to idle for at least five minutes before first disconnecting the black cable from the flat battery, followed by the live one. Repeat for the red cable.

● It is recommended you get the battery properly charged at the earliest opportunity.

how to
buy a used car

Buying a second-hand car is a big decision, and most of us don't really know what to look out for. Before you buy, you should run a vehicle history and valuation check (try www.aalemoncheck.co.nz), take it for a test drive and get a full mechanical inspection. But when you initially inspect the vehicle, here are a few things to take note of:

- Look at the body of the car in good light. Apart from obvious rust, scratches and dents, look for bubbles in the paintwork and evidence of filler used in rust holes. Look underneath for rust or evidence of repair.

- Check wear and tear on the interior — including rust on the floor span and damp smells and other odours, which may be difficult to get rid of.

car

● If the engine oil is milky, it might contain water — this is a sign of a blown head gasket. Check the radiator fins aren't rusted or crumbly and there are no leaks of water, oil or petrol.

● Push down on each corner of the car to check the suspension — the shock absorbers could be worn if it bounces more than twice.

● Check the tyre tread is deep enough and is worn evenly. Make sure the spare is in good condition and there is a good, working jack.

A complete checklist is available at www.consumer.org.nz.

how to
change your oil

It can be a messy job, but changing the oil in your car isn't complicated. Change it every 5000km or according to the manufacturer's instructions.

● Along with new oil, you'll need a filter, a wrench that fits, and a pan to catch the old oil you drain out. Ask at an auto-parts shop if you are not sure what equipment you need.

● Park your car on a flat surface and run the engine for a few minutes so that the warmed oil drains easily. Make sure the car is in first gear or park and that the handbrake is on.

● Wearing old clothes (latex gloves and protective glasses are also a good idea), place the pan under the drain plug of your oil tank and remove the plug, letting the old oil flow out. Replace the plug.

car

● Remove the old filter and pour out the old oil it holds into your pan. Dab some new oil around the top of the new filter before you screw it in, to make it easier to remove next time.

● Remove the oil cap and pour in the new oil to the level recommended in the owner's manual (use the dipstick to check).

● Check for leaks under the car, then start the engine and check again.

● Dispose of the old oil at a recycling service station or check with your council about what's advisable. Never tip it down the drain.

how to
save petrol

New Zealanders love their cars and have one of the highest rates of car ownership in the world. With petrol prices at an all-time high, it's wise to start applying a few simple rules to help you save on fuel.

- The most obvious tip is to use your car less. Walk short distances, combine as many errands as you can into one trip, and turn off your car if you have to stop for more than a couple of minutes.

- Keep your car running efficiently with regular tune-ups, and reduce drag by keeping the body streamlined. Only use roof racks when you have to. Keep your tyres inflated to the correct pressure and remove unnecessary weight from the boot and back seat.

car

● Drive smoothly. Avoid heavy acceleration and try to move quickly through the gears. Sudden braking will cause you to lose acceleration, so try to read what the traffic is doing and stay alert. Never drive over the speed limit on the open road — not only is driving under or to the limit safer, it's also cost-efficient.

● Turn off the extras. Air-conditioning consumes the most fuel, but also turn off your seat warmer and window demister when not in use.

● The AA recommends checking the price of petrol before you buy it and keeping your tank full to avoid being caught out should a further sudden price increase occur.

how to
change a car tyre

It's no longer fitting (let alone safe) for the modern woman to flag down a stranger to help change a tyre. And since a leak or a flat tyre inevitably occurs in a rainstorm or peak-hour traffic, everyone needs to know how to change it quickly and efficiently.

You need: a properly inflated spare tyre, a car jack, a wheel-brace and something to get your wheel cover off — like a screwdriver.

● Park the car on a hard, level surface. If you're on soft ground, put an object like a block of wood under the jack.

● Get everyone out of the car, turn the ignition off, put the handbrake on and the car in gear. (Seems obvious? You'd be surprised.)

car

● Hope like mad your wheel-nuts have not been over-tightened by the last person.

● Jack up the car (ensuring the jack sits under the car frame) until it's high enough to take the wheel off. Take off the wheel cover and the wheel-nuts. Put the nuts in a safe place.

● Take the wheel off and replace with the spare. Tighten wheel-nuts a little.

● Lower car, remove jack and fully tighten the wheel-nuts.

● Don't forget to have your spare repaired as soon as you can.

how to
parallel park

Parallel parking is one of the hardest driving skills to learn, and even experienced drivers muck it up sometimes. Remember these tips to save yourself the embarrassment of creating a traffic jam while you sweat and fret over getting into a park.

● Make sure you wait behind the space with your indicator on if the space isn't free yet. When it is, pull up parallel to the car in front with a bit more than half a metre of space between you and your rear bumpers aligned. If you are unsure whether your car will fit into a parking space, measure your car alongside it, remembering that you will need about a metre of extra space to compensate for the bits of the car you can't see.

car

- Make sure your indicator is still flashing, and check for pedestrians and other traffic before moving. Back slowly into the park with your steering wheel turned one full rotation towards the kerb, stopping when the back of the front door is in line with the bumper of the car in front. At this point, start turning the wheel away from the kerb, continuing to back into the park and making sure the side of your car doesn't scrape the other car.

- Stop about 30cm from the kerb, moving forward and back until you have an even amount of space between the cars in front of you and behind.

how to
use a semicolon

The semicolon is consistently misused. It is either wantonly wedged between random words or completely ignored. There is no reason for this indiscretion. The semicolon (symbolised as a comma with a dot above it) is an essential piece of punctuation; it's also very easy to use. Just learn the two main rules and never over- or under-semicolonise again.

● To connect two independent clauses: Independent clauses are series of words that can stand alone as complete sentences. When you want to connect two of them, use a semicolon. For example: This is a complete sentence; this could be another one. Note: Use a semicolon before a conjunctive adverb, but if there's a conjunction (like 'and' or 'but'), stick to a comma.

grammar

● The super comma: When you have a series of items that would normally be separated by commas except that each individual item already has a comma in it, you can use a semicolon instead. For example: My brothers were born on September 13, 1959; November 20, 1964; and January 2, 1966.

how to
speed-read

Lingering over a good book is one of life's pleasures, but there are times when you need to read and understand material quickly and efficiently. Most adults read 200–300 words per minute, but it is possible to read over 1000 without any loss in comprehension. Use these pointers to train your reading speed.

● Run your finger quickly across the page underneath the text or move a ruler or bookmark vertically down the page, making sure your eyes keep up.

● Read for concepts rather than individual words by widening your eye span. Try to make reading more of a visual experience like driving a car, taking in as much information as possible in a short amount of time. Notice key words — subjects, verbs and objects.

● Get rid of bad habits. Don't pronounce words in your head as you read and don't re-read passages. As a rule, the slower you read the more often you re-read, as your thoughts have more opportunities to wander.

● At first, speed-reading takes a lot of concentration. If your momentum is waning, take a moment to rest your eyes and recall the ideas in the passage you have just read.

how to
use an apostrophe

The apostrophe is a much misused item of grammar, yet the rules for its use are really pretty simple. The apostrophe turns up in two main instances — to denote contraction and possession (see below). An apostrophe is NEVER used to denote plurals.

- For contraction, i.e. merging two words into one, use the apostrophe to replace the missing letter. For example, 'it is' becomes 'it's', 'do not' becomes 'don't', 'they are' becomes 'they're', 'you are' becomes 'you're' (not to be confused with the possessive your — see below).

- To denote possession. For singular, put the apostrophe before the 's'; for example, 'one boy's hat'.

grammar

- Personal possessive pronouns do not take an apostrophe, for example your, yours, hers, its, theirs, ours. The exception is one's.

- With possessive plurals, use the apostrophe immediately after you have made the noun into its plural; for example, 'two boys' hats', 'two men's hats', 'the children's rabbit', 'the people's choice'.

- When in doubt, consult a good website, such as www.grammarbook.com.

how to
build your vocabulary

A large vocabulary is a powerful tool — not to be used for showing off, but rather for communicating more clearly and accurately, and being able to understand others better. Why use two words when you can use one?

● Reading more, and reading widely, are the most important things you can do to expose yourself to new words. But you must read actively — think about the meaning of each unfamiliar word, try to deduce what it means through context, and, finally, make sure you know what it means by looking it up in the dictionary. It helps to keep a list of your new words at hand if you want to revise them.

● Other ways to expose yourself to new words include playing word games, doing crosswords, reading the

thesaurus or even signing up to receive a 'word of the day' email from a website like www.dictionary.com or the *New York Times* (www.nytimes.com/learning/students/wordofday/index.html).

- About half the words in the English language are derived from Greek or Latin root words. Familiarise yourself with these root words and you will be able to grasp the meaning of entire groups of words much more quickly. Also learn the suffixes and prefixes.

- Once you've learned your new word, try to use it where appropriate. If you're not quite sure, try it out on friends or family first. Using the word in context will help cement it in your mind.

how to
handle a job interview

Few meetings in life are as pressured as the job interview. When we are desperate to make a good first impression, we can be easily intimidated by the occasion.

- To make a good impression, gather as much information as you can beforehand about the organisation and the interview itself — how long it will be, how many people will be present, and who they are. Ask for a copy of the job description so that you can tailor your answers to it. Go through lists of common questions, which are available on the internet.

- Interviewers don't like a candidate who doesn't ask questions. Don't wait until the end — go armed with a list of pertinent, genuine questions and ask them when it seems appropriate. It's OK to write them down. Avoid asking anything too obvious or rude (such as when you

can expect your first pay rise), and use the opportunity to ask what concerns the interviewer might have about you, so that you can clear them up.

- The little things make all the difference. Have clean hair, nails, clothes, shoes and teeth, and switch off your cellphone. Make sure you arrive on time. Ask what the next step in the process is and have them commit to a date by which they will make contact. Remember the interviewer's name, and send them a follow-up email thanking them for their time.

- After all the preparation, remember to let your personality shine through. The interviewer likes to know who they're dealing with.

how to
resign correctly

Whether you love or loathe your job, if possible you should always leave it on good terms. Once you have decided to resign, aim to make a graceful departure: act professionally, with courtesy and etiquette. Here are some guidelines:

● Write a letter to your boss. Keep it short and to the point with the date you plan to leave and your signature. It is best not to send it by email. There's something about a real letter that says 'this is serious'.

● Hand it to your boss personally when no one else is around.

● Make sure you have calculated your notice time exactly — double-check the terms in your employment agreement or contract. It's better not to get into a

wrangle over time owing when your boss may be miffed at your leaving anyway.

- Keep gloating about your new job to a minimum; don't disclose your new salary and perks unless you want to really get up people's noses. You might want a reference.

- Leave quietly without slamming doors. You never know when you might want or need to work with the same people again.

- Before you say too much about why you have chosen to take on a different job, consider whether or not you can afford to be honest. You might be better to stick to vague generalities, such as 'it's my dream job'.

how to
swing a golf club

It's commonly known that important deals can be made on the golf course — so even if you hate the sodding game, one day you might just need it. So how do you swing a golf club in a way that shows you mean business? Just concentrate on these three things:

● **Grip**
Lay the club handle diagonally across your left palm and close your fingers around it. With your right palm facing the direction you want the ball to go, close it over the left thumb to form a snug grip where you can see two knuckles of each hand. If you're left-handed, reverse.

out and about

● Stance

Your feet should be a little more than shoulder-width apart, slightly flared and with the club and ball aligned to your centre or slightly left of centre.

● Swing

Shift your body weight to your back foot in the backswing, twisting slightly and keeping your front arm straight and your back slightly bent. Transferring weight to your front foot in the downswing, hit the ball squarely and when you've finished, check that your back shoulder is over your front foot. Easy.

how to
light a campfire

There's nothing quite like sitting round a cosy fire after a day at the beach, or while camping in the great outdoors. Here are some tips to help you build a successful fire, and ensure it's properly extinguished when you've finished.

- Always have a shovel and a large bucket of water with you.

- Use a previously made rock fire ring or make your own in a space well away from trees or debris.

- Make a small, loose pile of tinder (for example, paper, small twigs or dry leaves) and build a cone of kindling wood and/or dry branches over the top.

● Touch a match to the tinder and discard it into the pile. You may need to blow it gently, but don't use starter fluid or flammable liquids. As the kindling burns down, add more until the fire is burning well.

● Gradually place on larger dry pieces or driftwood. Do this one piece at a time. Allow enough space for air to flow.

● Before you leave, allow the fire to die down to ashes. Pour water over it and stir with the shovel, getting deep into the pit to ensure any hot spots stop smouldering. Don't leave the site until the fire is completely cold. Check local bylaws before lighting any fire.

how to
bid at an auction

It's possible to buy almost anything at auction, from property to cars to antique furniture. The fast-paced bidding can be scary for first-timers, so it's a good idea to observe a few auctions before you take part in one yourself.

- Bidders at auctions must be cashed up or have finance arranged, as all bids are unconditional offers. It's important to do as much research as possible beforehand. Make sure you have things like builder's reports, title searches and mechanical checks, and familiarise yourself with the terms and conditions of the auction and negotiate changes if necessary. Inspect the property or item thoroughly prior to auction and get a feel for what the market's like so you know what to expect to pay.

out and *about*

● Be cool: you'll more often than not be bidding
  against one other person — so don't get caught up
  in the competitiveness of the moment and bid more
  than you can afford. And although we've all heard the
  horror stories, don't worry — an unintentional nose
  scratch won't be a legally enforceable bid.

● Online auctions have their own set of rules. Research
  the site, the seller and the item. Don't pay with cash
  or money order prior to delivery, or give your credit-
  card number out over the internet. Third-party payment
  services are the safest option.

how to
skip a stone

To the English it is 'ducks and drakes' and to the Danish it's 'smutting'. Whatever you call it, skipping stones on a calm patch of water is one of life's simplest pleasures. It is only frustrating if you've never been shown how.

- Hunting for the perfect stone to skip is half the fun. Look out for one that fits easily into the palm of your hand, is not too thick and has a flat, smooth surface. River stones are excellent.

- Hold the stone with the flat surface facing parallel to the ground, resting on your middle finger, which should be gently bent. Curl your index finger around the edge of the stone and have your thumb holding it down from the top.

The key to getting a stone to skip is to spin it rapidly so that it doesn't break the surface of the water, but instead hits it so as to create a little wave that it will bounce off. To do this, crouch side-on to the water and bend your elbow into your side. Bend your wrist back and then flick it forward as fast as you can, keeping the stone flat and sending it spinning like a disc towards the water. If you want to get really technical, a group of pointy-headed stone-skipping enthusiasts have found that for the maximum number of bounces the angle between the stone and the water should be about 20° from the horizontal.

how to
swim freestyle

Imagine a line running lengthwise through the centre of your body. To swim freestyle you need to rotate left and right around this axis — spending more time on your side than on your front.

- Keep your head low and your hips high, kicking quickly and strongly with your legs as close to the surface as possible without making big splashes. Kick from the thigh rather than the knee, keeping your leg straight.

- Move your arms in a slightly flattened windmill motion, bending from the elbow. When one bent arm is completely out of the water you should be twisting towards it, with your other arm beginning its movement

through the water. Once you have a good 'catch' of the water, try to visualise yourself levering your body past your hand and forearm, rather than pushing your hand past your body.

- Breathe out your nose. Take a breath with your mouth once every two or three strokes, when your body and face are twisted out of the water. Bilateral breathing (on both sides) will help you stay on course.

meet the grannies

Patsy Duffy The best advice Patsy ever received from another Granny was 'Never let the romance die.' That, and 'Don't be surprised when a red wine stain turns purple in the wash.' Those two tenets might or might not be connected. Patsy reckons the grannylode of all knowledge lies somewhere between the two but is happy to share experience on everything else gleaned from a life long lived.

Geraldine Johns — who writes under the *nom de plume* Hazel Bang for Granny — had to abandon her early aspirations to be a trapeze artist when she discovered she had a fear of heights. She turned to journalism instead. She has written for both local and international publications, in England, the United States and New Zealand. Now she tries to maintain a fine balance between full-time freelancing and the care of her young son.

Veronica Schmidt is a 30-year-old journalist with Granny-like tendencies. She was formerly the assistant editor of *Sunday* and has written for *Metro*, *The Listener* and the *New Zealand Herald*. She now lives in England.

Katie Newton is a freelance journalist who is currently working as the fashion and beauty editor for *Sunday* magazine. Despite compiling the 'Granny' column for over 18 months, she is about as domesticated as a Sumatran Tiger.

Bonnie Sumner is a writer and editorial assistant for *Sunday* magazine. She lives in Auckland with her partner and puppy and attempts to balance a homely Granny life with a tendency to party.

Jo Tronc has worked as an illustrator for 18 years and is based in Auckland, but works globally. She works in most areas of the industry — packaging, design, publishing, advertising, and does a lot of handcrafted typographic work. Jo also enjoys studying part-time short courses, and currently is enjoying photography, prior to that Global Politics!